New World, New Realities: The Remaining Roles of Government in International Telecommunications

A Report of the Fifth Annual Aspen Institute Roundtable on International Telecommunications

Rob Frieden
Rapporteur

THE ASPEN INSTITUTE

Communications and Society Program
Charles M. Firestone
Executive Director
Washington, DC
2000

To purchase additional copies of this report, please contact:

The Aspen Institute
Publications Office
P.O. Box 222
109 Houghton Lab Lane
Queenstown, Maryland 21658
Phone: (410) 820-5326
Fax: (410) 827-9174
E-mail: publications@aspeninstitute.org

For all other inquiries, please contact:

The Aspen Institute
Communications and Society Program
One Dupont Circle, NW
Suite 700
Washington, DC 20036
Phone: (202) 736-5818
Fax: (202) 467-0790

Charles M. Firestone
Executive Director

Amy Korzick Garmer
Associate Director

The Aspen Institute
One Dupont Circle, NW
Suite 700
Washington, DC 20036

Published in the United States of America in 2000
by The Aspen Institute

Printed in the United States of America

ISBN: 0-89843-277-4

Contents

Foreword

Ten years ago, who would have guessed that consumers would one day use computers to buy groceries, download music, or make long distance telephone calls? Turn on the nightly news or glance at the financial pages of any newspaper, the message is everywhere: Internet companies are revolutionizing the way we do business, virtually overnight.

As information technology becomes more widespread and accessible, consumers increasingly demand greater access to enhanced information services that enable them to make decisions in real time. For example, consumers in developed countries subscribe to mobile services to increase their flexibility and mobility. Likewise, consumers in developing countries rely upon mobile service to increase communications in areas where access to traditional voice services has been lacking, poor, or unreliable.

The implications of the information revolution reverberate throughout society and the global economy at all levels. The impact of the information revolution on the telecommunications industry has been particularly stark. Communications companies have facilitated extraordinary change over the past five years and are expected to spur even more remarkable change over the next three to five years. For example:

- According to a University of Texas study, one in three of the companies that constitute the present *Internet economy* did not exist in 1995. In 1999, Internet-based companies contributed roughly $507 billion to the U.S. gross domestic product.[1] On a global scale, industry experts estimate that global e-commerce will grow from U.S. $109 billion in 1999 to $1.3 trillion in 2003.[2]
- Internet telephony and wireless Internet access, in their infancy in the late 1990s, will continue growing rapidly. Analysts project that, by 2003, no less than 34 percent of U.S. households and 45 percent of U.S. business will be serviceable by broadband wireless networks.[3]

- As infrastructure expands, new voices are connecting to global networks. In Europe, for example, industry analysts project that Internet usage will increase from 33.9 million users at the end of 1999 to nearly 60 million users by 2003.[4] In that same time span, analysts forecast that Internet usage in Latin America will surge from 9 million to 38 million users.[5] Moreover, analysts estimate that Internet usage in Asia will grow from 21.8 million users in 1999 to 95.2 million users by year-end 2004.[6]
- Not only are new individuals getting onto the network, international communication is now accessible in countries where domestic communication has traditionally been difficult for technical or political reasons. For example, in Somalia, a country that has been embroiled in civil war for years, mobile phone subscribers can make international calls for a dollar a minute.[7]

As faster, better, cheaper, and smarter alternatives to wireline telephony become more widely available, communications traffic will continue migrating from the Public Switched Telephone Network to alternate networks largely based on wireless and Internet protocols. As increasing amounts of traffic are carried over these alternate networks and the Internet continues to drive the global economy, the current regulatory system—which was designed for a non-competitive telecommunications environment—needs to adapt to meet these new realities. The transformation of the global information and communications industry must be matched by changes in the regulatory and governmental elements of the system.

The 1999 Aspen Institute Roundtable on International Telecommunications

In this context, the Aspen Institute convened the Fifth Annual Aspen Institute Roundtable on International Telecommunications, June 27-30, 1999, in Aspen Colorado, to facilitate dialogue on appropriate roles for governments in the changing telecommunications landscape. Twenty-three government officials, executives of global communications and information companies, academics, and consumer representatives participated in the session.

Central to this conference report is a single assumption: Governments continue to have a role in the telecommunications sector, but that role needs to change. Instead of providing or guaranteeing services to their constituencies, governments will increasingly exercise pragmatic involvement. We will likely see governments limit their actions to narrowly targeted functions in three categories: creating, promoting, and maintaining competition in telecommunications, protecting users, and acting where the market cannot achieve legitimate social goals. The following report analyses the role of government in these functions. In the matrix below, for every function, three degrees of government involvement are considered: directive, laissez-faire, and something in between which we call a hybrid.

FIGURE 1: ROLE OF GOVERNMENT

TYPE OF GOVERNANCE	**Directive**	**Hybrid**	**Laissez-Faire**
FUNCTION OF GOVERNMENT			
Promote and maintain a market	State-owned monopolies	Limited government regulation of competitive markets, or industry self-regulation	"Invisible hand" regulates market
User protection	Government protects users against predatory, fraudulent, and abusive practices	Government relies on industry self-governance to develop and apply standards and compels disclosure to consumers	Courts settle contractual disputes between users and companies
Social goals (e.g., universal access)	Government subsidies inherent in pricing	Explicit, targeted subsidies	Underserved areas gain access when the market renders it feasible

Hybrid Governance Model of International Telecommunications

The most interesting aspect of AIRIT 1999 was that in each function, the new, hybrid approach to governance was favored. Instead of government owning, operating, or micro-managing the market, participants favored governments leveraging or channeling market and social forces. Participants used many different terms to get this across: a regulator of self-regulators, a harness for greed, or an aggregator of unattractive consumers into a pod large enough to be attractive to vendors. In sum: the hybrid model blends government reliance on market and social forces with limited, pragmatic involvement to achieve narrowly defined goals.

Although the report details these, and other, more specific suggestions, it is important to note that no votes were taken, and participants were not asked to sign any particular statements. Thus, the observations of consensus are those of the rapporteur and should in no way be construed as the statement of any particular participant or employer unless specifically noted as such. Furthermore, these suggestions and others debated at the AIRIT series are intended as suggestions to advance the dialogue and deliberation on these issues in other forums—not necessarily the definitive answers, but rather, models, new ways of thinking about the issues and beginning points.

Acknowledgments

There are numerous individuals whose commitment of time, intellect, and resources have made the Fifth Annual Aspen Institute Roundtable on International Telecommunications possible. First, we thank our rapporteur, Rob Frieden, professor of Telecommunications at Pennsylvania State University, who presents a useful framework—and a wealth of meaningful context—for understanding the issues discussed at the conference.

Second, we gratefully acknowledge the participants in the fifth annual meeting, whose names are listed in the appendix to this report, for their participation in the conference and for their follow-up afterward. Two conference participants merit special thanks: Stuart Brotman for moderating the roundtable and guiding the selection of conference readings, and Tedson Meyers for applying his superb editorial skills to this conference report. We also acknowledge our sponsors, without whose generous support this conference would not have been possible: Bell Atlantic, British Telecommunications North America, Cable & Wireless, GTE, Nippon Telegraph and Telephone, Nortel Networks, Oracle, Research Institute of Telecommunications and Economics–Japan, and U S West.

Additionally, we thank the staff of the Aspen Institute Communications and Society Program, in particular, Beth Wachs, program associate, for developing the conference and overseeing the production of this report; Patricia Kelly, senior program coordinator, for coordinating the conference; and Sunny Sumter-Sana, publications manager. We also thank Rebecca Weaver and Tyler Stone of the Aspen Institute Publications Office and David Stearman, copy editor, for their help with the production of this report.

Charles M. Firestone
Executive Vice President, Policy Programs
and
Executive Director, Communications and Society Program
The Aspen Institute

Notes

1. Anitesh Barua and Andrew B. Whinston, "Measuring the Internet Economy" (Austin, TX: The University of Texas and Cisco Systems, October 1999), available: http://www.internetindicators.com (last accessed December 8, 1999).

2. Business Software Alliance Press Release, "Regulatory-Free Cyberspace Necessary for Continued E-Commerce Growth" (Washington, D.C.: Business Software Alliance, December 1, 1999), available: http://www.bsa.org/pressbox/policy/944070474.html (last accessed December 8, 1999).

3. The Strategis Group Press Release, "Revenues in the Wireless Broadband Market Will Soar 418 Percent in Next Five Years, The Strategis Group Reports" (Washington, DC: The Strategis Group, December 6, 1999), available: http://www.strategisgroup.com/press/pubs/wbb99.html (last accessed December 8, 1999).

4. Forrester Research Press Release, "One In Three Europeans Will Embrace A Digital Lifestyle By 2003" (Amsterdam, Netherlands: Forrester Research, December 6, 1999), available: http://www.forrester.com/ER/Press/Release/0,1769,190,FF.html (last accessed December 16, 1999).

5. Jupiter Communications Press Release, "Jupiter Communications Initiates Efforts in Latin America with New Research Services, Industry Forum, and Sales Presence" (New York: Jupiter Communications, November 8, 1999), available: http://www.jup.com/company/pressrelease.jsp?doc=pr991108 (last accessed December 16, 1999).

6. International Data Corporation (IDC) Press Release, "IDC Sees Internet Boom Time for Asia/Pacific," (Framingham, Mass.: IDC, November 29, 1999), available: http://www.idg.com (last accessed December 8, 1999).

7. Mark Turner, "Lagging in the Information Revolution," Financial Times Survey: FT Telecoms, October 8, 1999: p. 32.

Introduction

New World, New Realities

Much has changed in the international telecommunications environment since 1995, when the Aspen Institute convened the first annual Aspen Institute Roundtable on International Telecommunications (AIRIT):

- The Internet has reached critical mass, with credible forecasts that data communications soon will predominate over voice services for the first time;[1]
- Internet-mediated telephone service has begun to challenge the traditional toll revenue-sharing arrangements and pricing systems based on voice services;[2]
- Regional and global market opening trade initiatives have become a reality;[3]
- Strategic industrial alliances have grown in importance as carriers strive to exploit new market access opportunities;[4] and
- Deregulation and market liberalization have become more widespread in developed and developing nations alike.[5]

At this last Roundtable before the millennium, participants concentrated on the way forward—with particular emphasis on recalibrating the roles and functions of government in international telecommunications. They accepted the view that technological innovations and changed philosophies have properly triggered a general trend toward less direct government involvement in telecommunications. They also agreed, however, that less governance does not mean no government whatsoever. Although some stakeholders may advocate the complete withdrawal of government in the telecommunications sector, such an exit appears politically infeasible. Given that public values depend on a healthy communications infrastructure, governments do not have the option of doing nothing.

Eli Noam, professor of finance and economics at the Columbia Business School and director of the Columbia Institute for Tele-

Information, dismissed the "no government" view as disingenuous. He noted that although "knee-jerk libertarianism" has cachet in some camps, many such "gunboat libertarians" seek their own deregulation while continuing to lobby relentlessly for regulatory safeguards applied to competitors.

The quest at this Fifth Annual Aspen Institute Roundtable on International Telecommunications focused on plotting a new roadmap for governance, fine tuned for improved performance and limited to areas where government can make a positive difference.

Higher Stakes, Bolder Initiatives

The upheaval in international telecommunications parallels the substantial change many nations have experienced domestically. It results, in large part, from the impact of technological change. When a nation fosters competition in the domestic sector by authorizing additional wireless, long distance, and local exchange carriers, both carriers and consumers eventually look toward similar opportunities for international services. Domestic and international competition typically fosters downward pressure on rates and unleashes pent-up demand.

Technological innovations have made it possible for competition to flourish because the barriers to market entry have declined and new services have proliferated. Consumers have embraced technological innovations by expecting more than "plain old telephone service" (POTS). The familiar migration from POTS to PANS ("pretty amazing new stuff") results from the successful introduction and consumer acceptance of technological innovations and services.

By 1999, several technological and political developments had reached critical mass. Telecommunications and information technology companies have incorporated digital technologies into their networks with an eye toward satisfying pent-up consumer demand for expanded bandwidth. The Internet has become the primary motivation for consumers to buy personal computers and demand high-speed access to the information superhighway.[6]

Governments have responded to changed technological circumstances and the requirements of their electorates. Within the past five years, nations representing more than 80 percent of global trade in telecommunication services have made significant commitments toward open market access under the auspices of the newly created World Trade Organization (WTO).[7] The European Union's "Big Bang" means that some nations already have begun to integrate markets and the networks needed to interconnect them.[8] The nations of the European Union also have agreed to consistent, equal, and transparent treatment of national and foreign ventures and open market entry in the telecommunications and information technology industries.[9]

After several false starts, the U.S. Congress in 1996 enacted a broad revision of the Communications Act of 1934 that reshapes both telecommunications policy and the regulatory mission of the Federal Communications Commission (FCC).[10] For its part, the FCC has pursued a robust and perhaps aggressive campaign to reform international telecommunications rules and regulations, including a controversial action to estimate the costs that carriers incur in providing service and prescribing rates that U.S. carriers and their foreign correspondents must use when providing service jointly.[11]

Wireless Ascendancy

Several participants emphasized the increasing importance of wireless technologies as a key vehicle to serve mobile applications and user interests in productivity enhancement and safety. Wireless technologies also can support business ventures in developing countries to replace, rather than augment, the wireline infrastructure. To illustrate this point, Rohan Samarajiva, director general of telecommunications for the Telecommunications Regulatory Commission of Sri Lanka, noted that over the past four years the cellular network in his country has expanded sixfold; by comparison, the wireline network expanded only threefold. Fixed wireless service can provide a means to deploy services more quickly, efficiently, and cheaply to both hinterlands and urban areas.

Even with rates of about 10 cents per minute in developing countries, however, metered wireless service may not achieve universal service goals without subsidies. Given this pricing scheme, universal access is more feasible for the occasional, expensive call than for universal service. If wireless technologies displace wireline networks as the dominant medium, a larger part of the world might fall within the footprint of service, yet may still lack funds to use it. Governments, arguably, cannot claim victory in having reached the social goal of universal telecommunications access simply because communications satellites illuminate the entire Earth and increasingly one or more terrestrial options exist in most locales. Thus, nations seeking to pursue universal service goals in rural and high-cost areas may want to consider technologically neutral policies, such as targeted subsidies, that create incentives for wireless carriers as well as incumbent wireline operators.

The Network of Networks

Marketplace developments have accelerated the pace of change in telecommunications and information services. The Internet has altered—at least temporarily—tried-and-true methodologies for determining value. Run-ups in stock market prices of ventures such as eBay, E*trade, Amazon.com, Cisco, and America Online attest to the enthusiasm and optimism that the Internet generates. It seems that virtually any venture can enhance its valuation and perceived commercial promise by adopting a name with an "e" prefix (denoting electronic commerce) or a ".com" suffix (denoting a commercial presence on the Internet).

For example, Izumi Aizu, principal of Asia Network Research, reported that Above Net, Inc.—a company with limited physical assets that was formed three years ago by three people with $400,000 in seed money—achieved a $400 million valuation through an initial public offering and was quickly acquired for $1.9 billion. Because the Internet facilitates direct commerce between businesses, as well as among consumers and businesses, the market value of Above Net may prove appropriate. That valuation took into account the expectations of consumers and investors on future earnings. Above Net's value exceeds by one-third the value of International Digital Communications of Japan[12]—a venture with substantial physical assets, including the transmission and switching capacity that make Internet-mediated communications and commercial transactions possible.

The widening gap in stock valuation between telecommunications and information companies may reflect more than euphoria over the Internet and a "gold rush" mentality. Clay T. Whitehead, president of Clay Whitehead Associates, commented that stock markets in the aggregate rarely "get it wrong"—leading him to wonder whether telecommunications soon may evolve into a commodity business. Telecommunications may become an enabler with fungible building blocks upon which other companies add value. Under this scenario, telecommunications carriers would operate more like utilities: enabling, but neither driving nor adding value to, business applications.

Suddenly—or so it appears—the Internet industry has solved perennially troublesome physical and financial impediments, making possible the "ascendency of ideas over infrastructure." Some technological futurists, such as George Gilder, believe that transmission capacity—the building blocks for telecommunications and information services—will cost so little that carriers need not meter service and charge on the basis of use.[13] Even if this view underestimates future costs, an upgraded digital telecommunications infrastructure offers the promise of enabling, rather than impeding, Internet-mediated commerce and the ability of entrepreneurs to hatch an idea, secure ample venture capital, and bring that idea or solution to a global market.

On the other hand, the current infrastructure still has limitations, bottlenecks, and irritations. Marc Rotenberg, executive director of the Electronic Privacy Information Center, noted the inadequacy of even the latest forms of dial-up access to the Internet. For consumers to have complete access to the full array of goods and services available via the Internet, telecommunications operators must digitize their networks and offer broadband first and last mile connectivity.[14] Despite the expectation that consumers want and will pay for such access, carriers need more on which to prepare a business case for investing billions of dollars in infrastructure upgrades. Virginia Sheffield, assistant vice president for regulatory/client services–international of GTE Service Corporation, noted limitations in predicting which technological innovations will satisfy market demands. Technology stimulates more competition and greater risk, with opposite consequences.

The former tends to trigger the perception of a need to act quickly, whereas the latter evokes reluctance to invest in any particular technology as an "early mover" until better and more complete data supports a particular roll-out strategy.

Hiroshi Kometa, vice president of the network business division of Nippon Telegraph and Telephone Corporation, corroborated this point. Although telecommunications carriers do not wish to miss out on market opportunities, they have to consider the consequences of making more investments, possibly in the wrong technology—particularly in light of having recently deployed new facilities that must generate revenues for many years before reaching their tax, accounting, or technological end of life. Other participants noted the reluctance of many companies to pursue, for example, third generation wireless technologies until concensus had been reached on standards and investments in second generation systems had been recovered.

The Internet Comes of Age

At some point in the late 1990s, the Internet became the primary driver for the changes necessary to hasten the onset of an information age economy. One such change is increased investment—by telecommunications carriers in transmission capacity and by consumers in personal computers and other information devices.[15] Even as blue-sky prognosticators continue to extrapolate and project future accomplishments, the current Internet actually has delivered on the mantra of "faster, better, cheaper and smarter." It has reached what Andrew Grove terms the "strategic inflection point"[16] (or critical mass), for a number of reasons.

In a nutshell, the Internet has developed into a major communications and commercial medium because other long-touted concepts also became real and provided the foundation on which to build a thriving international network of networks.[17] The Internet could not become a vibrant and credible medium without:

- proliferation of high-bandwidth capacity to house, deliver, and route desirable content to a large and geographically diverse population;

- technological innovations that promoted the convergence of previously discrete media and services;
- wise decisions, made by governments, encouraging new technologies without regulating and managing Internet applications; and
- creative entrepreneurs, activists, and citizens of cyberspace who trigger innovations and buzz, attracting more users at all levels.

Rising Importance of Packet Switching and the Internet Protocol

Several participants offered convincing arguments that the Internet will change virtually all current notions about the technology and regulation of international telecommunications 5 to 10 years hence. For example, telecommunications carriers and information service providers increasingly find that they can recover facilities-based investments on the basis of fixed, rather than mileage-based, rates. Distance insensitivity means that information service providers need not meter traffic, price service as a function of distance, or impose higher rates simply because traffic crosses national borders. Long usage sessions typical of World Wide Web surfing (in contrast to short holding times for voice conversations) are forcing network planners to accommodate greater demand and to provide new services. Moreover, the low-bandwidth requirements of voice telephony will no longer dominate and drive network design and engineering.

Most participants agreed that the telecommunications/information infrastructure must accommodate exploding consumer demand for digital throughput. Accommodation must occur regardless of whether or when data will overtake voice in total traffic volume and bandwidth requirements. Clay Whitehead referred to the development of the internet (with a lowercase "i")—the technological infrastructure—as evidence that consumers and business already require flexible, broadband networks.[18] The lowercase internet makes it possible to deliver the uppercase Internet—the content, services, and features that are available from the infrastructure.

Today's voice-oriented public switched telephone network (PSTN) does not always serve emerging consumer requirements because of the narrowband, analog local exchange loops that serve end users and the need for modems that take minutes to configure. Many forecasters expect major infrastructure upgrades to occur over the next 5 to 10 years. Cheaper bandwidth will supply affordable broadband pipes for multimedia applications and Internet services.[19]

Some carriers, such as Qwest and Level Three, already have configured international networks to accommodate Internet traffic. If these new ventures are proven right, a network based on Internet mediation will predominate. Carriers will convert conventional voice transmissions into packets and route them over diverse, space-available capacity using TCP/IP: Transmission Control Protocol (TCP) to handle network management and Internet Protocol (IP) to handle origination and destination addressing and numbering. Although some participants noted quality-of-service problems in the Internet's current "best efforts" routing topology, others expressed confidence that Internet-mediated "virtual circuits" will evolve to assure quality, reliability, security, and billing.

Trouble in Paradise

Amid the promise and broad optimism for telecommunications and information technology lurks the potential to deepen the digital divide. The Internet and its related infrastructure may accommodate nations and individuals already doing well, leaving countless billions untouched by the information revolution. Not everyone will have an opportunity or reason to tap into terabit pipes. The local first and last mile remains a problem in most countries. Fewer than 30 percent of the world's population, even in developed countries, have bought on-line access.[20] Seemingly endless sources of information are available in one language—English—85 percent of the time. Moreover, the fast pace of change can strand investment bases. Less developed nations may leapfrog intermediate technologies. Still, no nation can entirely avoid the consequences of installing cutting-edge technology only to find it obsolete—but not fully depreciated—two years later.

The pace of change and heightened potential for dislocation

present a quandary. Telecommunications can evolve into an enabling technology, rather than a costly impediment to progress. Entrepreneurs have an opportunity, as never before, to shorten the cycle between idea and market debut. Yet telecommunications and information technologies can empower only where they exist. Throughout the Roundtable discussions, many participants acknowledged the dilemma of unequal access to such services—a dilemma unlikely to find a market-based, technological, or government-generated solution. Despite the leapfrogging promise of wireless and satellite technologies, infrastructure needed universally to access the Internet remains out of reach. One region's pent-up demand that remains unsatisfied by technological upgrades becomes another region's missed opportunities.

Rohan Samarajiva expressed concern that developing countries might miss out on much of the technological and marketplace progress, for two reasons. First, enterprises with the capital and know-how to develop and improve national infrastructures might consider smaller markets not worth the risk of time, money, and effort. Second, many residents and regulators in developing countries are wary of electronic commerce and information technologies. Many people in these nations have yet to enjoy reliable plain old telephone service. Still others cannot afford supplemental services, for which they would have to pay high, usage-sensitive rates.

Juanita Gana Quiroz, vice minister and undersecretary of telecommunications for the Chilean Ministry of Transportation and Telecommunications, noted that government can respond by creating an environment that is conducive to direct foreign investment and innovation. Chile's procompetitive policies stimulated infrastructure investment, market entry, and downward pressure on rates. The result: the unleashing of pent-up consumer demand for equipment and services.

Roundtable participants viewed the current situation as mixed and not entirely appealing. On one hand, a broader and diversified technological pallet provides greater promise for eliminating infrastructure concerns and increased access to broadband capacity at reasonable, possibly distance- and usage-insensitive, rates. On the other hand, preexisting dichotomies (Northern

Hemisphere/Southern Hemisphere; rich/poor; developed/developing) may grow more pronounced; as a result, billions of people still may lack access to basic communications technologies.

Financing the Information Revolution

In most industrialized nations, there appears to be no shortage of money, ideas, and appetite for tapping into the rich vein of opportunity created by the Internet. Stock may appreciate threefold on the first day of trading, drop sharply days or months later, and perhaps surge again as experts and pundits question old methods for valuing these ventures and assets. The rising tide of stock and cash in the Internet economy has not reached all locales, however. The recession in Japan and a continuing scarcity of venture capital in many developing nations offers a sobering counterpoint to the perception of limitless opportunity.

Financing infrastructure upgrades has great importance for three primary reasons. First, to narrow the gap between information rich and poor, developing nations need capital on favorable terms. New technologies may then enable developing nations to leapfrog and close the gap with developed nations. Conversely, lack of capital will put vital electronic commerce and other Internet-mediated transactions beyond reach for developing nations. Second, development of telecommunications and information technology industries may become key missions for bankers of last resort, such as the World Bank. Such development may also assure life-sustaining mandates for intergovernmental organizations such as the International Telecommunication Union (ITU). Third, many sources of venture capital view competition, market entry opportunities, and regulatory reform as attracting and supporting increased investment in the telecommunications sector.

In an Internet-centric world, electronic commerce and trade matters may dominate where regulatory concerns once prevailed. The ITU's portfolio, clout, and legitimacy are at stake. The ITU has begun to articulate an agenda for development and training in developing nations. Absent such a new mission, the ITU might have little to offer beyond spectrum management—a painfully slow standard-setting process typically overtaken by market forces—and the offering of its "good offices" for conference and event planning.

What's a Government to Do?

If technology, entrepreneurship, and consumer demand constitute bottom-up drivers of change, then government policy operates from the top down. Governments can trigger significant change by legislating competition from new, facilities-based carriers. Privatization of incumbent carriers and liberalization of the rules under which they operate can foster efficiency gains. Governments increasingly recognize the strategic importance of telecommunications and information processing to a nation's overall economic health. Few nations can tolerate and sustain the social and economic losses resulting from the failure to revise and revamp—if not jettison—anachronistic rules, policies, and regulations.

In the old world order, governments owned or pervasively regulated the telecommunications sector because of its importance to national security, under the prevailing view that competition in this sector would prove disruptive and harmful to the national interest. Such assumptions derived from the sense that a single carrier could operate most efficiently as a natural monopoly. Competition would result in wasteful duplication of facilities in urban locales, do nothing to achieve universe service objectives, and fragment limited sources of capital for infrastructure upgrades.

The new telecommunications order displaced that economic rationale with the support of solid empirical data. Telecommunications, like information processing, typically does not support or require a single natural monopoly. Competition has proven a stimulant for innovation, investment, and consumer satisfaction. A robust array of interconnected and competing networks actually supports reliability and sustains development.

Roundtable participants devoted substantial time to the goal of articulating a recalibrated and refined mission for government. Significant changes in government telecommunications policy helped shape a competitive marketplace, where previously most governments had centrally managed the industry sector. Many nations now embark on steps that trendsetting countries undertook several decades ago to foster resale and facilities-based competition. For their part, the early movers must continuously fine-tune the scope, function, and tools of government to enhance the benefits of competition and attain still greater social benefits.

The Role of International Telecommunications in Our Communities

This section of the report will examine telecommunications and the Internet and their role in our private and public lives. It also will consider how the mantra "faster, better, cheaper, smarter" drives entrepreneurs to bring new, innovative services to market. Moreover, it will examine how the concept of convergence became real and how the Internet became a legitimate and growing medium for international commerce.

The Mantra

If the Internet changes everything, as some advocates claim, then sophisticated, high-speed telecommunications and information processing applications must reach into the homes, hearts, and computers of most people. To reach such a mass market, robust international broadband networks must exist to make it possible for Internet companies to market products and services on a near-ubiquitous basis. In turn, consumers willingly must pay for these goods and services using various currencies—including cash, credit, and attention (the eyes and ears that broadcasters broker to advertisers).

Consumers flock to the Internet presumably because it provides desirable services in innovative, entertaining, and user-friendly ways. But Internet-mediated services generate repeat patronage after an initial period of curiosity and intrigue if and only if such services improve on what previously available services have offered. The slogan "faster, better, cheaper, smarter" identifies some of the key features telecommunications and information technology must have in order to find and sustain market share. Although the services need not offer improvements in each category, on balance, users should perceive a qualitatively better outcome.

At their highest value, new and enhanced services, including the Internet, can change the balance of power in favor of the consumer. They afford access to information (e.g., automobile prices). They enable use of that information to prompt sellers to compete more vigorously (e.g., evidence of a car buyer's qualifications and serious intent to purchase a fairly priced vehicle). The Internet can expand the scope of both a buyer's search and a seller's geographical reach. This medium threatens the ability of intermediaries to mark up prices, but it also can enhance the role of intelligent intermediaries who can parse, process, and prioritize boundless information.

Faster

Internet time operates 24 hours a day, 7 days a week. With time and distance becoming irrelevant, Internet-mediated commerce accelerates many transactions, triggers efficiency gains, and reduces costs as fewer chains of marketing, management, inventory, and customer care are required.

Compare, for example, on-line air travel reservation systems and human travel agents. Internet-mediated reservation systems exist now (e.g., Expedia; Travelocity; Cheap Tickets, Inc.; and Priceline.com). Once past the learning curve, the user has access to much of the search and ticketing power and control previously available only to travel agents. In short order, travelers can book air transportation, use strategies to reduce cost or maximize comfort (e.g., the ability on some reservation systems to examine available seating options). Travelers can also avoid telephone tag with agents and can acquire electronic tickets for greater convenience.

The Internet-mediated option excels, however, only if the consumer knows how to maneuver through various reservation systems, confident that security and authentication procedures will safeguard privacy. But drawbacks exist. On-line reservation systems may not offer the best available fares or disclose all available options in an unbiased manner. A variety of factors could slow the transaction: for example, Internet congestion, narrowband telephone lines, server capacity, or limitations of ISP facilities (number and speed of modems). On balance, where the traveler does not need the advice and perspective of an agent, Internet mediation provides a faster and more efficient option. It shortens the link between consumers and airlines by enabling geographically disbursed consumers to tap into the speed, data warehousing, and processing capabilities of computers.

Better

People will differ in their perception of what makes something qualitatively better. Few newspaper readers, for example, might consider Internet mediation by itself an improvement, as it takes time to download content and to maneuver from page to page. Other enhancements to the Internet version, however, may change the calculus (e.g., almost real-time updates, keyword searches, and customizing features).

"Better" also may entail an era of transition in the way people absorb information. Currently, Internet mediation requires the conversion of content into what we perceive as an attenuated visual and auditory context. Transmission bottlenecks commonly foreclose full motion displays in certain markets. Current display monitors and speakers are limited in their ability to reproduce images and sounds. Nevertheless, the Internet provides consumers with substantially more options and the opportunity to explore virtually any interest. If better means more, then access to thousands of Web-based newspapers, news sites, and news radio programs provides greater opportunities to stay informed. If knowledge means power, then the Internet can empower almost anyone with the ability to acquire data and information. Knowledge, however, still requires individual, noncomputerized, processing skill.

Cheaper

The Internet can streamline, economize, and render more efficient almost any transaction. The World Wide Web increases in value to consumers, advertisers, and sellers with each additional site. Economists describe this characteristic as accruing positive networking externalities—that is, increasing value and utility to users of the medium while the cost of use and the cost per user stays the same or falls.

Internet-mediated transactions may be cheaper for consumers, who can eliminate intermediary markups by cutting out middlemen and dealing directly with suppliers. In turn, Internet-based suppliers—whether actual producers or mere purchase order aggregators—can exploit the Internet to reduce inventory to just-in-time levels and align production to consumer demand. Thus, a clothing manufacturer that relies heavily on Internet-mediated transactions can quickly change production runs to produce more of a favored size, color, or style in accordance with customized purchase orders. For their part, advertisers may achieve lower exposure costs while reaching selective audiences.

Smarter

Information technology entails the power of computers to store, process, and search through massive amounts of data. Artificial intelligence, data mining, intelligent agents, and a host of information management techniques provide Internet users with evolving tools to work, play, and learn smarter. Artificial intelligence provides ways for computers and the Internet to respond and adapt to individual interests and requirements. Coupled with intelligent agents, Internet services can canvass and cull through massive amounts of information to collect what an individual wants to see. Data mining and other search tools provide better ways to understand consumer behavior.

Consumers can further enhance the value they derive from the Internet by linking its vast array of information, commercial, and entertainment sources to information processing functions. For example, on some online auction sites a bidder can activate a proxy bidding option to raise bids as needed up to a bidder-imposed cap. This feature replaces frequent monitoring of the bidding process by enabling automatic bid revisions when necessary.

The Rule of Four C's

If the "faster, better, cheaper, smarter" mantra comes across as narrowly technological, consider Internet-dominated international communications in the context of four key descriptive words: content, community, commerce, and convenience.

Content

For people intent on acquiring information (e.g., stock market prices), the Internet delivers content in a faster, better, cheaper, and smarter way. Stock prices can arrive in real time, rather than on a delayed basis (e.g., yesterday's closing prices in the financial pages) or the historical electronic price of 20 minutes past. Access to real-time share prices empowers users, particularly when such access joins with the ability to buy and sell on-line at the current price level with lower transaction costs. Through the Internet, on-line traders also have access to countless statistical and analytical aids in real time—on-screen data previously available only to industry professionals.

Community

The targeting and aggregation of consumers serve immediate and long-term marketing goals. In the short run, the development of portals and special-interest Web pages allows suppliers to lock in enough consumers to support specialized commerce. For example, the Internet can help geographically dispersed consumers with narrowly shared interests to obtain goods and services formerly offered only in large cities (e.g., a bookstore dedicated to mysteries or science fiction, or a source for a particular china or silverware pattern).

In the long run, the development of Internet sites targeting narrow groups develops a new element of community and shared interests not easily achieved through mass marketing. The Internet, coupled with information processing capabilities, makes it possible for even modest providers of goods and services to learn more about their customers and their needs.

What providers can do by way of data mining and analysis, consumers can do by becoming better-informed and savvier customers. Some providers may not encourage consumers to trade notes, but others willingly provide such a forum and serve as honest brokers, reaping rewards as a result. Consumers tend to linger at Web sites that provide personal value along with opportunities for like-minded people to communicate. Travel sites that add information about destinations, along with reservation and ticketing functions, tend to develop repeat business. Such functions generate consumer trust and confidence and perhaps, over time, a sense of community. Large-volume book sellers such as Amazon.com hope that the combination of data mining and community building will engender the same consumer goodwill as do coffee bars in local or franchised outlets.

Commerce

Commerce drives the Internet's growth, which in turn stimulates demand for bigger telecommunications networks to transport burgeoning Internet traffic. User demand turns into billions of dollars in computer and router sales of companies such as Dell and Cisco, as well as the thousands of dollars accrued by individual stock market day traders and home-based sellers of Beanie Babies and other collectibles. Currently, the Internet provides a medium for, at most, a few percentage points of commercial transactions, including those relying on Internet mediation (e.g., sales of airline tickets, books, and shares in stock). The future promises enormous commercial activity stemming from the current growth rate and the robust diversification of services and functions performed.

Convenience

Consumers prefer Internet mediation when it saves time, money, and effort. Increasingly, the Internet reduces hassles and offers greater convenience. The Internet can provide price information, canvass sellers, offer desktop previews to replace fruitless trips, and provide home-based opportunities for replacing routine outings (e.g., grocery purchases). The Internet provides countless case studies in which cleverness and creativity offer ways to enhance the quality of life, reduce drudgery, and expand leisure opportunities.

Toward Sustainable Competition in International Telecommunications

This section of the report will examine telecommunications competition in the context of a three-stage journey that many nations have taken, or will take, over time. State-owned monopolies operate at the starting point of our competition road map. The endpoint has full facilities-based competition, with limited government regulation targeted to serve narrow and defined functions (e.g., enforcement of antitrust and consumer protection laws). Not all nations currently have ideal economic and political conditions for reaching the endpoint identified here. Our map, however, can help track a nation's progress toward that goal.

This section also examines new roles for governments in the three distinct stages of telecommunications competition. It outlines several objectives for government in nations where telecommunications competition is strong: implementing hybrid telecommunications governance models based largely on public-private partnerships, eliminating technology-based regulation, and responding to market failures.

How Did Competition Appear in This Sector?

For generations, economists, regulators, legislators, judges, and most observers accepted the notion that telecommunications sectors could not support competition. Phrases such as natural monopoly, market failure, foreign attachment, and national security were common. In all nations, few believed that marketplace forces had any place in the sector, or offered any promise for consumers. Indeed, the prevailing view considered competition potentially harmful. Surely, market entrants would "creamskim" their way to profitability by serving large-volume customers, leaving the incumbent with low-volume subscribers and the duties of universal access. At the very least, government had to manage the sector, if not own and operate the carriers, lest consumer welfare decline or sovereignty and national security be threatened.

In such a noncompetitive environment, government must assure services, subsidize rural and high-cost areas, and attend to the poor and elderly. At times, heavy-handed "command and control" regulation seeks to remedy carrier and market shortcomings. Under such circumstances, governments have a stake in maintaining the status quo. It would take a revolution in economic theory or politics to trigger change.

Such revolutions have occurred peacefully, with dynamic consequences. Over time, monumental changes in politics and macroeconomics—coupled with substantial technological innovation, changed cost structures, and reduced financial barriers to market entry—have precipitated change in telecommunications policy. Political responses to these economic and technological drivers—Thatcherism, Reaganomics, the economic theory of market contestability, unbundling, and new legislation or treaty commitments—have triggered dramatic change and unleashed the power and creativity of entrepreneurship to identify and serve pent-up demand.

In the early 1980s, the Thatcher government in the United Kingdom followed deregulatory initiatives undertaken in the United States, leading to initial procompetitive steps such as separating telephone service from the lease of telephone handsets, which allowed competition to evolve in the latter sector.[21] For the first time, consumers could purchase their own telephones from a wide variety of suppliers rather than having to accept a one-size-fits-all, black rotary unit.

The Three Stages of Competition Policy

Stage One

In the 1980s, procompetition advocates had few supporters around the globe. At the time, policy makers viewed U.S. and U.K. initiatives as isolated excursions. On the European continent, U.K. overtures were termed "the English disease," and many policy makers aggressively resisted competition. The fear of competition went beyond the mere defense of tradition. The perceived stakes centered on the consequence of meddling with a major employer (often the government itself) and a powerful mass of employees, not only unionized but at times the largest single union in the land. The high stakes triggered extreme caution and fears about the unknown. They included concerns about destructive competition and premonitions that the public would suffer in the long run if competition and price reductions proved unsustainable. Would a competitive environment imperil public policy objectives? Policymakers expressed concerns about the effect of competition both on consumers and on employees of the incumbent carrier—many of whom would lose their jobs as the company streamlined to meet competition.

Stage One telecommunications competition policy commences amid such misgivings. Thus, its character leans toward the hesitant and experimental. Little empirical evidence existed in the 1980s to support the deregulation of the telecommunications sector in general, including the liberalization of rules applicable to the incumbent carrier. In Stage One competition, decision-makers respond to fundamental changes in political philosophy and cost structures as well as mounting business pressure from outside the telecommunications sector.

Even in the United States, where private enterprise predominated, many people objected to the divestiture of AT&T and other procompetitive initiatives. Incumbent stakeholders clung to the status quo and exercised significant political clout to block change. Private industry voiced the majority of the objections. One branch of government, the Department of Defense, also raised objections on the basis of national security concerns.

Government officials often trigger Stage One competition policy on their own. Policy shifts responding to real or perceived public mandates for change are common, especially when accompanied by a change of leadership in the executive or legislative branches of government. The Reagan and Thatcher administrations embraced competition. Both promised less government—and delivered on that promise.

Elsewhere, "less government" party platforms led governments to abandon ownership or control of industrial sectors—including telecommunications, transportation, natural resources, and utilities. Privatization sparked by Stage One competition responds to political concerns for mounting deficits and taxes. It provides new opportunities for the private sector to attempt strategies aimed at lower prices, higher profits, and greater efficiencies.

Typically, in response to privatization, governments explore new regulatory mechanisms, either within traditional ministries or as independent regulatory authorities. Where political will is sufficient, this is a task of legislatures, not heads of state. Alternatively—as in the United States—the courts may also play a major role, either in framing the basic change or in interpreting legislation. No legislation can anticipate every contingency, and stakeholders bent on delay will explore loopholes. Thus, the setting for Stage One telecommunications competition may first manifest itself in the courtroom, not in the marketplace. For example, the FCC has incurred substantial delays in implementing the Telecommunications Act of 1996 as federal court litigation has redirected the Commission's staff resources. Rather than execute Congressional intent, the FCC and other interested parties have battled over what Congress intended.

Stage Two

The next stage in telecommunications competition policy features entrepreneurial creativity and actual market entry in some sectors. In Stage Two competition, regulators guide competition rather than resisting it. Governments typically permit market entry in market niches with relatively low technological and financial barriers. These activities include resale of the incumbent carrier's facilities and basic services; adding value to and enhancing leased lines; and marketing (but not manufacturing) end-user equipment, such as handsets and private branch exchanges.

At Stage Two, competition advocates grow bolder. They press to tilt policy in favor of market entrants by obligating the incumbent carrier to facilitate competition. When they succeed, common carrier rules force incumbents to interconnect facilities and to permit resale. They must offer network functionality to newcomers as an *à la carte* menu of service elements at cost-based prices, significantly below the retail rate. In return, the legislature or regulatory agency may open new market opportunities to the incumbent contingent upon the emergence of true, sustainable competition in existing markets. The incumbent carrier also may leverage its experience and size for global outreach, forming new strategic partnerships to acquire market share and revenues abroad, offsetting what it will lose to competitors at home.

To remain viable, Stage Two telecommunications competition entails a balance of regulation and enterprise. On one hand, Stage Two requires governments to adopt policies permitting resale of incumbent carrier facilities. Newcomers must make substantial investments in new facilities, which users need to meet near-term and growing demand for services, without duplicating embedded capacity. On the other hand, regulators—whether new or seasoned—should find themselves assuring market entry, suppressing abuses, and doing both with maximum forbearance.

The changing telecommunications sector will operate in flux during this stage. In response, governments run the risk of "accordion regulation": lagging behind the marketplace, then micromanaging the sector to catch up, based on the mistaken view that imperfect competition requires government intervention to come closer to a preconceived economic model. During Stage Two, regulation can become asymmetric: one template for the incumbent and another for new market entrants.[22] In a transition to full and robust competition (Stage Three), asymmetric regulation help for a defined period. Absent a clear timetable for sunsetting the imbalance, however, inconsistent regulation may handicap unfairly the incumbent carrier with no public benefit.

Asymmetric regulation can promote great uncertainty and thus delay the migration to Stage Three telecommunications competition. It triggers the already keen instinct to protracted litigation and raises doubts about policy direction. Current examples of asymmetric regulation in one Stage Two nation (the United States) include:

- imposing common carrier obligations on telephone companies—requiring the unbundling of network service elements with *à la carte* pricing—while exempting cable television operators from similar duties even when they use the cable television network to provide functionally equivalent telecommunication services;[23]

- requiring interexchange carriers to pay above-cost local exchange access fees, coupled with a duty to help fund universal service subsidies, while exempting ventures that use the same type of access to originate and terminate a blend of basic (functionally equivalent) and value-added services; and
- allowing an Internet service provider (ISP) to form a local exchange carrier that exclusively handles the ISP's traffic, thereby qualifying the carrier for compensation from the incumbent local exchange carrier without any prospect that reciprocal traffic and compensation will flow back to the incumbent carrier.

Stage Three

Stage Three telecommunications competition policy represents a theoretical end point: Robust, facilities-based competition would thrive in all sectors of the telecommunications industry. Conventional government regulation largely would be unnecessary.

To date, no nation has reached Stage Three. In some nations (e.g., New Zealand), marketplace conditions do not necessarily support competition in all sectors. In others (e.g., the United States and the United Kingdom), deregulatory initiatives remain incomplete. Accordingly, the examination that follows in this Report explores prospective transitions from Stage Two to Stage Three telecommunications competition.

A New Role for Government

Although a global trend toward competition has clearly occurred, its nature and scope will vary among nations. Our three-stage model merely identifies a path that many nations may follow. Some nations will pursue Stage Three competition vigorously; others will avoid it altogether. An added policy factor bears consideration: International telecommunications requires multilateral cooperation. Accordingly, once a nation reforms its domestic policies it will need to coordinate change regionally and globally.

Regardless of whether and how governments promote competition in telecommunications, the nature and scope of regulation inevitably must change. Private capital and the infusion of newcomers make certain a new cultural perspective that emphasizes business goals and discipline. A clash of cultures surely will occur. The incumbents' orientation blends business with public service, accepts government regulation as a necessary evil, and negotiates ways to capture the regulator, invoking their own regulated status to thwart competition. Newcomers arriving from unregulated environments may resist government oversight, or dodge it by entering through content-dominant commerce, such as the Internet. Some newcomers also may use government regulation of the incumbent carrier to further their own interests. Governments should exercise extreme caution to maintain regulation that serves competition, as opposed to regulation that upholds the interests of a subset of competitors.

Amidst this clash of competitors, governments will have responsibility to optimize economic and social welfare. To maintain an appealing environment for market entry and robust competition, governments must change their missions and functions. New functions will include nullifying moves that retard competition or diminish the public benefits of this new environment. In effect, governments must transform themselves—becoming promoters of competition instead of micromanagers of a captive industry. At no stage, however, does government exit the regulatory arena completely. Libertarian visions of a government-free telecommunications sector fail in two respects: They overlook governments' obligation to extract public benefits from the system, and they make no distinction between past practice and new, narrowly drawn government roles. In a market progressing toward full competition, government operates within a limited, reliable matrix rather than a vague, endless mandate to promote the public interest. In such a market, government turns over that mandate to competition and then monitors practices and results.

The pace of change, however, is hardly even. Technologies forge ahead; competitors race to respond. Governments can never match them, move for move. Regulatory bias has telling consequences. Detailed and entrenched, regulation remains burdensome. Streamlined and limited, it fuels market entry and public rewards.

Developing a Hybrid Model of Government

Substantial empirical evidence demonstrates that marketplace competition and balanced regulation serve the public interest in the international telecommunications environment. Balanced regulation is imperative. On one hand, competition thrives where technologies and entrepreneurs can freely find markets and where governments resist the temptation to intervene (ostensibly to level the competitive playing field). On the other hand, governments' noninvolvement could imply indifference, which could harm consumers and prevent market entrants from securing full and fair interconnection with incumbent carriers. Absent effective antitrust enforcement, undesirable predatory practices could occur.

Accordingly, the primary objective articulated at the Fifth Roundtable involved the formation of a hybrid model. In this model, government both facilitates competition and incubates new technologies. For example, U.S. government bodies—such as the Defense Advanced Research Project Agency and the National Science Foundation—supported the Internet in its early stages of development. The same government, however, left the resulting technologies in the hands of market competitors. The process involves pragmatic involvement: Regulators must make conscious choices in determining what they should do on the basis of where they are needed most and what they do best.

Eliminating Technology-Based Regulation

Roundtable participants agreed that such a hybrid regulatory model could accommodate the reality of technological and marketplace convergence.[24] Governments could eliminate the anachronistic silo approach of compartmentalizing technologies and then adopting technology-specific regulations. That practice supported an era of experimentation, scarcity, and monopoly. Conduit, not content, predominated.

Traditional regulatory models based on broadcasting, cable television, and telephony (common carriage) do not serve well in an era when multiple technologies provide functionally equivalent services. For example, in both the developed and developing worlds alike, modern wireless telephony offers fixed services previously exclusive to wireline carriers. Similarly, the Internet and cable television can provide telephone services. Hence, traditional markets lose mutual exclusivity. Failure to update regulatory contexts can produce winners and losers not truly representative of market performance.

Mark Roellig, executive vice president for public policy, human resources and law at US West, underscored this point. He observed that the current style of regulation in many nations creates winners and losers independent of marketplace tests. According to Roellig, in a broadband marketplace, the rules must align with the services offered and apply equally without regard to technology, corporate longevity, or market share.

The hybrid regulatory model should enable technologies and services to reach markets rather than shield ventures from competition. To encourage competition and market rollout of new technologies, governments may advocate spectrum reallocation. They must enforce existing rules rather than sustain or expand the regulatory environment.[25] They must enforce those rules in an effective and timely manner to assure a level and predictable playing field for operators. They must prevent stakeholders from gaming the regulatory process to achieve delay or inconsistent outcomes or the preservation of a regime that is no longer justified.

The hybrid regulatory model must be flexible to ensure that an operator is not handicapped because of its incumbency or historical (and shrinking) market share. Nor should government foreclose foreign investment.[26] Rather, the hybrid model targets consumer welfare by fair and transparent rules of the road, a bias in favor of open market entry, and licensing of multiple operators.

Responding to Market Failure and Deficiencies in Self-Regulation

Throughout the world, a stated preference for unregulated telecommunications gives way to varying degrees of government involvement. Government oversight responds to:

- the reality or perception that the marketplace alone cannot achieve all social goals;

- industry consolidation or market dominance by one enterprise that may stifle competition; or
- self-regulation that might prove ineffective in some areas (e.g., consumer protection and antitrust enforcement).

Accordingly, most observers and stakeholders endorse or acknowledge the inevitability of government involvement in such diverse areas as antitrust enforcement, spectrum allocation, law enforcement, national and personal security, foreign relations, consumer protection, and the pursuit of acceptable social goals such as universal service. Even the Internet—regarded by some observers as a libertarian's paradise—cannot escape some degree of government involvement. The hybrid regulatory model assures narrow parameters for such involvement, however, and safeguards against well-intentioned zealots.

Consistently, it appears that nations have less difficulty deciding what to do than how to do it. The easier part involves the decision to open the telecommunications sector to market forces. The harder lies in sustaining competition as circumstances and markets change. This approach requires forbearance no less than it requires vigilance. It establishes a preference for self-regulation in much the same way as the U.S. Securities and Exchange Commission relies on securities markets to create and enforce rules and to discipline violators. In this model, governments intervene only where clear need exists (e.g., when industries cannot agree on standards of readiness for the year 2000).

Governments might have to intervene when stakeholders cannot reach consensus on a common standard or network interface (e.g., the domain registration process and numbering regime for the Internet); when stakeholders experience gridlock on shaping important industry-wide policies absent the threat of government intervention; or to mandate the "sunsetting" of existing regulations on a date certain. In sum, many nations have reined in government and fostered fuller interplay of market forces. The next steps involve close scrutiny of what goals competition will achieve and what roles remain for government in that context.

Working Group Deliberations and Recommendations

Working Groups at the Fifth Annual Aspen Institute Roundtable on International Telecommunications explored the role of government in the context of promoting competition, providing protection to users, and achieving societal goals. All groups addressed four fundamental issues:

1. What are governments' goals and responsibilities in the new world of competitive international telecommunications?
2. How do authorities know when these goals have been achieved? What are the guideposts?
3. What role should governments play—along a spectrum ranging from direct management to *laissez-faire*—over the medium to long term? Who within and across governments should play those roles?
4. How should the transition be handled? How should consumer needs be filled in the interim?

Despite the likely flaws in predicting even the near term for telecommunications, the Working Groups narrowed their discussions to the next 5 to 10 years. The groups offered insights on how technological innovations will shape the marketplace. They also acknowledged the impossible—identifying solutions to perennial challenges (e.g., defending consumers from unscrupulous ventures and approaching universal access even as social expectations of what constitutes basic lifeline services expand).

Participants' visions of the future—some just short of science fiction—generated optimism for technology in developed and developing nations. Participants expect substantial infrastructure improvements, which would accommodate higher bandwidth and throughput requirements for high-speed applications (e.g., full-motion video). Improvements largely should eliminate capacity shortages for long-haul routes. In developed nations, cable television modems, digital subscriber links, and wireless (terrestrial and satellite) transmission should expand options for local origination and termination of traffic—often termed the "first and last mile."

Competition

The Competition Working Group explored the development of a hybrid government regulatory model by constructing a chart separating the new and old world orders. This Working Group anticipated the containment of conventional telephony and broadcast regulation. Over time, this regulation would diminish in importance as technology and services evolve.

Figure 2: Stages of telecommunications Regulation

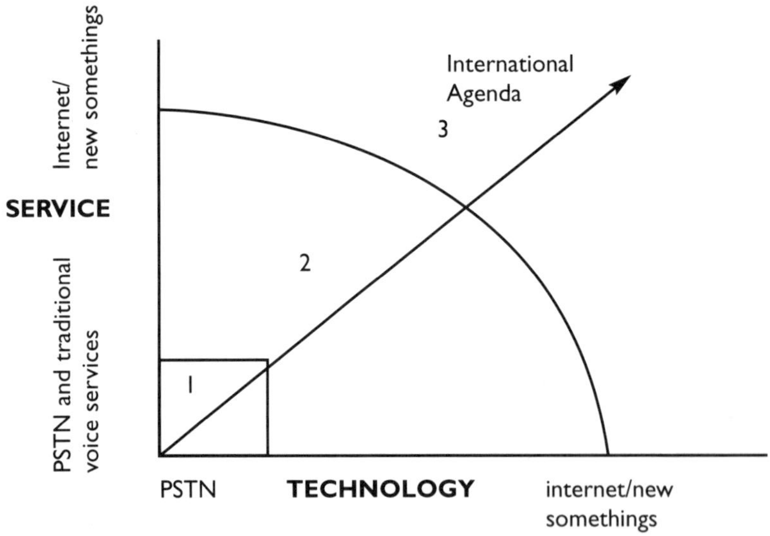

The box at the lower left represents the relative importance of the conventional public switched network and conventional broadcast television and their changing regulatory paradigm. Within the box, government has needed to impose traditional rules and regulations addressing interconnection, entry, rates, licensing, access to spectrum, and other social objectives (including universal service). Even here, however, government will reduce, over time, the scope of oversight and impose timetables for further deregulation. Government will migrate from "command and control" regulation, or from central management and ownership of the monopoly carrier, to a less intrusive approach. Government recognizes that, despite its good intentions, telecommunications regulation has become cumbersome, stifled innovation, thwarted direct foreign investment, and treated operators inconsistently. Government also recognizes that concern for user protection and societal issues leads the PSTN-oriented regulator to overemphasize competition issues and operate from assumptions of perfect competition articulated by lawyers and economists. Such assumptions may impel the regulator to micromanage the sector, often by implementing cross-subsidies.

Government also comes to recognize that the PSTN regulatory style poorly serves stakeholders who provide or consume Internet services. Such regulation continues to focus on the conventional PSTN despite the incentive to expand and cover Internet communications and electronic commerce. With the proliferation of new services and competing networks, PSTN-style regulation may become obsolete and unnecessary. The need for government stewardship, however, does not end. Rather, it shifts toward greater emphasis on user protection and ensuring competition (e.g., through antitrust enforcement and divestiture of the telecommunications regulatory portfolio from a sector-specific agency to multiple agencies with limited and selective jurisdictions).

The Competition Working Group suggested that an Internet-centric telecommunications and information services environment—particularly electronic commerce—will raise a host of new and challenging problems inviting some degree of government involvement. The expertise required, however, would be varied and would extend well beyond traditional sectoral regulation. Competition policy and antitrust enforcement would lie with the U.S. Justice Department (or its counterparts in other countries). Consumer protection would fall to the Federal Trade Commission (or equivalent ministries in other countries), departments of education, or rural development program managers. Electronic commerce will raise a variety of law enforcement issues, many of them novel—inviting government involvement to preserve financial integrity and privacy.

Although the Competition Working Group recommended a diminished role for government in the telecommunications sector and the divestiture of functions from a single sector-specific agency, it also acknowledged that some nations may maintain a need for sectoral regulatory agencies. Representatives from developing nations, including Juanita Gana Quiroz, voiced opposition to the near-term divestiture or diminished scope of authority of telecommunications regulatory agencies across the board. The transition to competition in developing nations, she argued, will require the direct involvement and full-time attention of a single sectoral agency with the necessary clout and resources to compel corporate compliance with regulatory requirements.

For developing nations, the pace of the reduction and diffusion of regulatory responsibilities may be slower, as domestic realities dictate. Government might not compel structural separation of the PSTN from other Internet applications. It might lack adequate antitrust enforcement power. Nevertheless, the Competition Working Group noted that, in the long run, most nations favor a lighter degree of regulatory oversight, particularly after successful market penetration by new services such as mobile telephony.

User Protection

The User Protection Working Group acknowledged that consumers of telecommunications and information services will demand government safeguards against predatory, fraudulent, intrusive, and abusive practices. Public support for market-based policies rests, in large part, on the popular perception that the Internet is a safe, user- and family-friendly medium. The Working Group recognized that the Internet will trigger new user concerns—such as concerns about individual rights to privacy amidst technologies that facilitate intrusions (both in e-commerce and in e-mail).

The Working Group recommended that national governments respond with baselines for user protection in the Internet-dominant sector and electronic commerce environment. The Organization for Economic Cooperation and Development (OECD) has considered consumer protection guidelines, but such safeguards should avoid trade and market access concerns. The agency charged with this portfolio needs a broad approach and a light hand. The Working Group suggested that the agency consider:

1. the need to address Internet and electronic privacy concerns;
2. the roles the Internet can play to promote civic participation and citizenship;
3. the encryption policy in terms of both enhancing privacy and foreclosing unnecessary governmental surveillance of private, noncriminal activities; and
4. the broad consumer protection issues raised by electronic commerce.

Thus, the Working Group concluded that government could not relinquish its user protection role to private regulation or the marketplace. Instead, the Working Group envisaged "regulated self-regulation," in the manner of stock exchanges: Governments would rely on industry self-governance to develop and apply safeguards. Because cyberspace defies conventional legal jurisdiction, government action must address criminal conduct. Government should compel full disclosure of information to consumers so they can make informed choices (e.g., health and safety choices raised by prescription medicine purchases through the Internet).

As part of its oversight, government would also become a role model. It may benchmark best practices to show how governments can protect consumers. It may also use new information technologies to improve its services, enabling better citizen participation in government-managed electronic transactions (e.g., motor vehicle registration).

Societal Goals

The Societal Goals Working Group shared the Roundtable's consensus that government should encourage private development of modern communication systems to enhance social opportunities. In that context, government roles would neither decline in importance nor lose merit. Rather, they would change to free up market forces.

In this Working Group's view, government would maintain a predictable and fair regulatory regime. It would clearly articulate actions it would undertake to serve social goals not met by private initiatives. It would provide stakeholders with a transparent regulatory process. Government would support a level playing field, favoring no competing technology or category of stakeholder. It also would facilitate or compel uniform standards and network interoperability to reduce user costs and promote ubiquitous access.

This Working Group concluded that governments will meet social goals only by tailoring regulation to the prevailing political and economic environment. Where society favors market forces, government must channel these forces and create incentives ("harness greed"). It can incubate technologies, promote entrepreneurship, and support small businesses. As a major user of telecommunications and information technologies, it can lead by example and encourage market entry to fuel its demand for goods and services. In all instances, government can tailor regulation to prevent market dominance or predatory practices. The Societal Goals Working Group also favored government benchmarks to showcase the use of empowering technologies such as the Internet.

Conclusions: The Remaining Roles of Government in International Telecommunications

The Fifth Annual Aspen Institute Roundtable on International Telecommunications reached several conclusions, some of which initially seem inconsistent. On one hand, Roundtable participants adopted a consensus view that government must back off from micromanagement. Instead, government needs hybrid models that blend a reliance on market forces with limited involvement, targeting narrowly defined goals. On the other hand, participants expected increasing government attention as the Internet becomes a center for social, political, and commercial transactions. Although many of these issues predate the Internet, they will grow along with it in complexity and importance. Governments simply cannot afford to ignore such concerns.

The Roundtable participants addressed several of those issues—such as privacy, electronic citizenship, and the balance between national security concerns and individual interests—but proposed no solutions. Other issues fell between self-regulation and government involvement. Among these were cybercrime and cyberlaw; fraud and truth in lending and billing; and the digital divide between individuals who can access and use modern information technologies and those lacking the access and skills to do so.

Rather, the Fifth Roundtable focused on a framework for government roles, going forward. Participants concluded that in the future, governments should adopt a facilitator role, rather than continue to act as a service provider, service guarantor, or constituency benefactor. Taxing one service to cross-subsidize another should be considered anachronistic absent compelling public policy justifications. Creating incentives for private enterprise to narrow the digital divide provides a better and more productive model. Moreover, government intervention in every real or perceived market failure constitutes an outdated and counterproductive strategy. New and effective: narrowly marshalling resources; creating tax incentives; countering concentrated power; and encouraging innovation, competition, and consumer options.

Roundtable participants agreed that the suggested role would require governments to curtail their regulatory impulses, set dates certain for sunsetting market-countervailing regulations, and apply resources narrowly to enforce rules and sustain competition. In essence, participants accepted the premise that governments cannot be all things to all people. The hybrid government model outlined here compels a triage of priorities—retaining some goals for government and deferring others to industry and the marketplace.

Roundtable participants agreed that the roles of governments must change. Governments cannot maintain the regulatory status quo. Current deregulatory paths in some nations are proceeding with astute recognition of the advantages of sharing responsibility with the marketplace. In other nations, the pace of change remains slow. There, governments have failed to make room for marketplace competition and have failed to deal with market failure, rule violations, or vacuums in public policy.

Overwhelmingly, evidence sustains the view that procompetitive telecommunications policies enhance consumer welfare. Nations refusing to embark on some procompetitive track have become a declining minority. The remaining role of governments entails liberalization and deregulation—retaining, however, fuel power to curb abuses, enhance the economy, and protect national security.

Roundtable participants recognized that new roles for government would best evolve slowly, with restraint. Headline-grabbing initiatives compel reaction and uncertainty. Privatizing the incumbent telephone company, issuing mobile carrier licenses, and generating some degree of facilities-based competition do not assure investment or innovation. More difficult, but no less essential, are smaller safeguarding initiatives that help sustain competition, promote public policy objectives such as universal service, and guard consumers against illegal and unsavory business practices. That approach requires finesse and forbearance. Newly minted regulators may favor more aggressive involvement—or none at all.

Ample support exists for the view that *laissez-faire* should constitute the appropriate default position for government regarding telecommunications, information processing, and the Internet. Even devout libertarians have come to recognize, however, the necessity of some regulatory involvement to achieve public acceptance of important evolving services. For this reason, creative public-private regulatory solutions have emerged (e.g., e-commerce groups established by Microsoft, IBM, and others). Another example of an innovative regulatory approach occurred in Europe, where industry self-regulation was quite useful in addressing cyber-porn and similar public policy concerns.

In view of the ongoing need for safeguards even in a competitive marketplace, the majority of Roundtable participants this year favored a potentially more effective governmental role: what the User Protection Working Group termed "regulated self-regulation." This model places government in a standby mode, ready to intervene only if self-regulatory actions and market-based corrections do not suffice. In this context, government can stick to what it does best and operate as the regulator of last resort.

Notes

1. Grant Lenahan, "Next Generation Networks: A Practical View of Network Evolution," available: http://www.telcordia.com/newsroom/knowledgebase/index.html (last accessed December 20, 1999); T.M. Denton Consultants, "Netheads versus Bellheads: Research into Emerging Issues in the Development and Deployment of Internet Protocols," Final Report for the Federal Department of Industry, Ottawa, Canada (1999), available: http://www.tmdenton.com/netheads.htm (last accessed December 20, 1999).

2. Robert M. Frieden, "Dialing for Dollars: Will the FCC Regulate Internet Telephony?" *Rutgers Computer and Technology Law Journal,* vol. 23, 1997, pp. 47–79 (1997).

3. John J. Alissi, "Revolutionizing the Telephone Industry: the World Trade Organization Agreement on Basic Telecommunications and the Federal Communications Commission Order," *Connecticut Journal of International Law,* vol. 13, Spring 1999, p. 485; Taunya L. McLarty, "Liberalized Telecommunications Trade in the WTO: Implications for Universal Service Policy" 51 *Federal Communications Law Journal,* vol. 51, December 1998, p. 1; Laura B. Sherman, "'Wildly Enthusiastic' about the First Multilateral Agreement on Trade in Telecommunications Services," *Federal Communications Law Journal,* vol. 51, December 1998, p. 61; Arthur E. Appleton, "Telecommunications Trade: Reach out and Touch Someone?" in Symposium: Linkage as Phenomenon: An Interdisciplinary Approach, *University of Pennsylvania Journal of International Economic Law,* vol. 19, Summer, 1998, p. 209; Paula Barnes Sours, "The Impact of U.S. Regulatory Activity on Prospects for Implementation Of the WTO Agreement on Basic Telecommunications," *North Carolina Journal of International Law and Commercial Regulation,* vol. 23, Summer 1998, p. 645; Stefan M. Meisner, "Global Telecommunications Competition a Reality: United States Complies with WTO Pact," *American University International Law Review,* vol. 13, 1998, p. 1345.

4. John H. Harwood II, William T. Lake, and David M. Sohn, "Competition in International Telecommunications Services," in "Symposium: Telecommunications Law: Unscrambling the Signals, Unbundling the Law," *Columbia Law Review,* vol. 97, May 1997, p. 874; Doug Galbi and Chris Keating, *Global Communications Alliances,* (Federal Communications Commission, International Bureau, February, 1996), available: http://www.fcc.gov/ib/ (last accessed December 20, 1999); Peter Drahos and Richard A. Joseph, "Telecommunications and Investment in the Great Supranational Regulatory Game," *Telecommunications Policy,* vol. 19, No. 8, 1995, pp. 619–35.

5. Ingo Vogelsang, "Micro-Economic Effects of Privatizing Telecommunications Enterprises," *Boston University International Law Journal,* vol. 13, Fall 1995, pp. 313-328 Jeffery Atik, "Technology and Distribution as Organizational Elements Within International Strategic Alliances," *University of Pennsylvania Journal of International Business Law,* vol. 14, Fall 1993, pp. 273-313; Meheroo Jussawalla, "Is the Communications Link Still Missing?" *Telecommunications Policy,* vol. 16, no. 6, July, 1992, pp. 485–503; Muhammad I. Ayish, "International Communication in the 1990s: Implications for the Third World," *International Affairs,* vol. 68, no. 3, 1992, pp. 487–510; Peng Hwa Ang, "The Causal Relationship Between Telecommunications and Economic Development: Cause for Re-Analysis," paper presented at 44th Annual Conference of the International Communication Association, (Sydney, Australia July 11-15, 1994); Heather E. Hudson, "Telecommunications and Development Ten Years After the Maitland Report: The Need for New Policies and Strategies," *Proceedings of PTC'94,* 1994, 69–78; Sam Pitroda, "Development, Democracy, and the Village Telephone," *Harvard Business Review,* November-December 1993, pp. 66–79.

6. For a comprehensive and helpful introduction to the Internet, see Adam Gaffin, "EFF's Guide to the Internet, v. 3.20" (December 11, 1996), available: http://www.eff.org/pub/Net_info/EFF_Net_Guide/netguide.eff (last accessed December 20, 1999). A concise and straightforward jurist's summary is available in Reno v. American Civil Liberties Union, 521 U.S. 844, 117 S.Ct. 2329 (1997), available: http://www2.epic.org/cda/cda_decision.html (last accessed December 20, 1999); see also the lower court's equally helpful summary at 929 F.Supp. 824, 64 U.S.L.W. 2794 (E.D. Pa. 1996).

7. The WTO was created by the Marrakesh Agreement Establishing the World Trade Organization, 33 International Legal Materials 1125 (1994). See also World Trade Organization, Council for Trade in Services, "Decision on Commitments in Basic Telecommunications," S/L/19 (adopted April 30, 1996); Final Report of the Negotiating Group on Basic Telecommunications, S/NGBT/18; William J. Drake, Rapporteur, *Toward Sustainable Competition in Global Telecommunications: From Principle to Practice, A Report of the Third Annual Aspen Institute Roundtable on International Telecommunications,* (Queenstown, Md.: The Aspen Institute, 1999); World Trade Organization, "The WTO Negotiations on Basic Telecommunications: Informal Summary of Commitments and M.F.N. Exemptions," March 6, 1997, available: http://www.wto.org/wto/new/bt-summ3.htm (last accessed December 20, 1999); World Trade Organization, Group on Basic Telecommunications, Report of the Group on Basic Telecommunications, S/GBT/4 (February 15, 1997); World Trade Organization, "Guide to Reading the GATS Schedule of Specific Commitments and the Lists of Article II (MFN) Exemptions," available: http://www.wto.org/wto/new/guide1.htm (last accessed December 20, 1999).

8. The "Big Bang" specifically refers to an agreement by European stock exchanges to quote security prices in the Euro, thereby aligning and coordinating many banking functions within the region.

9. See, e.g., European Commission, Directorate General-Information Society, "Status Report on European Union Telecommunications Policy," INFSO/A/1, (Brussels, 25 November 1999), available: http://www.ispo.cec.be/infosoc/telecompolicy/en/tcstatus.htm (last accessed December 20, 1999); see also Mark Naftel, "Countdown to 1998: Status of Telecommunications Competition in Europe and Comparison with the United States," *Journal of Transnational Law and Policy Fall,* vol. 7, 1997, p. 1.

10 .See Telecommunications Act of 1996, P.L. 104-104, 110 Stat. 56, codified at 47 U.S.C. §§ 151 et seq. (1996); M. Cimatoribus, A. De Tommaso, and P. Neri, "Impacts of the 1996 Telecommunications Act on the U.S. Model of Telecommunications Policy," *Telecommunications Policy,* vol. 22, no. 6, 1998, p. 493; Robert M. Frieden, "The Telecommunications Act of 1996: Predicting the Winners and Losers," *Hastings Communications & Entertainment Law Journal,* vol. 20, no. 1 Fall 1997, pp. 11-55.

11. See International Settlement Rates, IB Docket No. 96-261, Report and Order, 12 FCC Rcd. 19,806 (1997) (establishing four transition periods for compliance with settlement benchmark rates and responding to the potential for expanded opportunities for one-way bypass of an accounting rate settlement), *aff'd sub nom.* Cable & Wireless PLC v. FCC, 166 F.3d 1224 (D.C. Cir. 1999). The ITU's cost estimates corroborate the FCC's calculations. See International Telecommunication Union, *Direction of Traffic: Trends in international telephone tariffs,* (Geneva: ITU/Telegeography, 1996), available: http://www.itu.int/inset/whatare/dot/chap.2.htm (last accessed December 20, 1999) (reporting that the per-minute cost for routing an international telephone call via an INTELSAT satellite, including operating expenses, is US $0.02 and that factoring all switching, routing, interconnection, and administrative costs—including license fees,

advertising, and taxes—"the average per-minute cost of an international call is probably around $0.25."). See also Organisation for Economic Co-operation and Development, Committee for Information, Computer and Communications Policy, "New Technologies and Their Impact on the Accounting Rate System," OECD/GD(97)14 (Paris, 1997); Rob Frieden, "The Impact of Call-Back and Arbitrage on the Accounting Rate Regime," *Telecommunications Policy,* vol. 21, no. 9/10, 1997, pp. 819–27; Rob Frieden, "Falling Through the Cracks: International Accounting Rate Reform at the ITU and WTO." 22 *Telecommunications Policy,* vol. 22, no. 11, December 1998, pp. 963-975.

12. See Cable & Wireless IDC, World Wide Web site at http://www.idc.co.jp/english/index.html (last accessed December 20, 1999).

13. George Guilder, "The Bandwidth Tidal Wave Forbes ASAP, December 5, 1994, available: http://www.seas.upenn.edu/~gaj1/bandgg.html (last accessed December 20, 1999).

14. For background on issues pertaining to residential access to broadband networks, see Robert M. Entman, *Residential Access to Bandwidth: Exploring New Paradigms,* report of the Thirteenth Annual Aspen Institute Conference on Telecommunications Policy (Queenstown, Md.: The Aspen Institute, 1999).

15. For background on the technology, business, and economics of the Internet, see generally Kevin Werbach, *Digital Tornado: The Internet and Telecommunications Policy,* Federal Communications Commission, Office of Plans and Policies Series No. 29 (Washington, D.C.: March 1997), available: http://www.fcc.gov/Bureaus/OPP/working_papers/oppwp29pdf.html (last accessed December 20, 1999); Thomas M. Siebel and Pat House, Cyber Rules (New York: Currency/Doubleday, 1999); Kevin Kelly, *New Rules for the New Economy:* 10 Radical Strategies for a Connected World (New York: Viking/Penguin, 1998); Carl Shapiro and Hal R. Varian, *Information Rules: A Strategic Guide to the Network Economy* (Cambridge, Mass.: Harvard Business School Press, 1999).

16. "A strategic inflection point is a break in a curve where the old way of doing business gives way to a new way of doing business, where the old concepts and the old constructs transition into new concepts and new constructs and, at this point, a business, a society—or, for that matter, individual—can make that adjustment to the new or continue to work harder and harder with greater determination in the old way. The first one will rise to new prominence, new prosperity; the second one will lead to decline." Andrew S. Grove, Plenary Speech at World Economic Forum, February 3, 1997, Davos, Switzerland, available: http://www.andygrove.com/intel/people/asg/asg_davos.htm (last accessed December 20, 1999); see also http://www.intel.com/intel/paranoid/ (last accessed December 20, 1999).

17. See Eli M. Noam, "Beyond Liberalization—From the Network of Networks to the System of Systems," *Telecommunications Policy,* vol. 18, no. 4, 1994, pp. 286–94.

18. See International Telecommunication Union, *Challenges to the Network Telecoms and the Internet* (Geneva: 1997); Organisation for Economic Co-operation and Development, Directorate for Science, Technology and Industry, Committee for Information, Computer and Communications Policy, Working Party on Telecommunications and Information Services Policies, *Internet Traffic Exchange: Developments and Policy,* DSTI/ICCP/TISP(98)1 (1998).

19. For a helpful annotated bibliography of materials addressing Internet economics issues, including interconnection and access pricing, see Bruce Klopfenstein, "Internet

Economics: An Annotated Bibliography," *Journal of Media Economics,* vol. 11, no. 1, 1998, pp. 33–48.

20 See International Telecommunication Union, *World Telecommunication Development Report 1998,* Chapter 4, Universal Access: *Challenges to the Network Telecoms and the Internet* (Geneva, Switzerland: ITU, 1996).

21. The right of customers to attach acoustic devices to their telephones was established in Hush-A-Phone v. United States, 238 F.2d 266 (D.C. Cir. 1956), on remand sub nom. Hush-A-Phone v. AT&T, 22 FCC 112 (1957).

22. See Antonio Perrucci and Michela Cimatoribus, "Competition Convergence and Asymmetry in Telecommunications Regulation," *Telecommunications Policy,* vol. 21, no. 6, 1997, pp. 493–512.

23. For extensive analysis on this topic, see Barbara Esbin, *Internet Over Cable: Defining the Future in Terms of the Past,* Federal Communications Commission, OPP Working Paper Series No. 30 (August 1998), available: http://www.fcc.gov/Bureaus/OPP/working_papers/oppwp30.pdf (last accessed December 20, 1999).

24. Participants in other future-looking forums share this view. See International Telecommunication Union, "Chairman's Report of the Sixth Regulatory Colloquium, Regulatory Implications of Telecommunications Convergence," (Dec. 11–13, 1996), available: http://www.itu.int/itudoc/osg/colloq/briefrep/ (last accessed December 20, 1999); see also European Commission, "Green Paper on the Convergence of the Telecommunications Media and Information Technology Sectors, and the Implications for Regulation: Toward an Information Society Approach," COM(97)623 (Dec. 3, 1997), available: http://www.ispo.cec.be/convergencegp/97623.html (last accessed December 20, 1999).

25. An FCC Working Paper released in July 1999 endorses this premise. See Jason Oxman, *The FCC and the Unregulation of the Internet,* Federal Communications Commission, OPP Working Paper Series No. 31, available: http://www.fcc.gov/Bureaus/OPP/working_papers/oppwp31.pdf (last accessed December 20, 1999).

26. See Eli M. Noam and Anjali Singhal, "Supra-National Regulation for Supra-National Telecommunication Carrier?" *Telecommunications Policy,* vol. 20, no. 10, 1996, pp. 769–87.

APPENDIX

Fifth Annual Aspen Institute
Roundtable on International Telecommunications

List of Conference Participants

June 27–30, 1999
Aspen, Colorado

Izumi Aizu
Principal
Asia Network Research

Keith E. Bernard
Senior Vice President
Regulatory Policy
Cable and Wireless

Stuart N. Brotman
President
Stuart N. Brotman Communications
and
Research Fellow
Harvard Law School

Melanie Carter-Maguire
Director
Government Relations–International Trade
Nortel Networks

Charles M. Firestone
Executive Director
Communications and Society Program
and
Executive Vice President
Policy Programs
The Aspen Institute

Robert Frieden
Professor of Communications
Pennsylvania State University

Juanita Gana Quiroz
Vice-Minister
Undersecretary of Telecommunications
Chilean Ministry of Transportation and Telecommunications

Kelley Gannon
Director
International Government Affairs
Bell Atlantic Corporation

Note: Titles and affiliations are as of the date of the conference.

Hiroshi Kometa
Vice President
Network Business Division
Nippon Telegraph and Telephone

Eric H. M. Lee
Public Policy Director
Commercial Internet eXchange (CIX)

Tedson J. Meyers
Partner
Coudert Brothers

Susan Ness
Commissioner
U.S. Federal Communications Commission

Michael Niebel
DG-XIII
European Commission

Eli Noam
Professor of Finance and Economics
Columbia Business School and
Director
Columbia Institute for Tele-Information

Robert Pepper
Chief
Office of Plans and Policy
U.S. Federal Communications Commission

Kenneth G. Robinson, Jr.
Telecommunications Attorney

Mark Roellig
Executive Vice President
Public Policy, Human Resources & Law
General Counsel and Secretary
U S West

Marc Rotenberg
Executive Director
Electronic Privacy Information Center

Rohan Samarajiva
Director General of Telecommunications
Telecommunications Regulatory Commission of Sri Lanka

Note: Titles and affiliations are as of the date of the conference.

Virginia Sheffield
Assistant Vice President
Regulatory/Client Services–International
GTE Service Corporation

Herbert Ungerer
Head of Telecommunications, Postal Services, and Information Society Issues
DG-IV, European Commission

Clay T. Whitehead
President
Clay Whitehead Associates

Hironobu Yumoto
Deputy Director
Technology Policy Division
Communications Policy Bureau
Japanese Ministry of Posts and Telecommunications (MPT)

Staff

Beth I. Wachs
Program Associate
Communications and Society Program
The Aspen Institute

Patricia K. Kelly
Senior Program Coordinator
Communications and Society Program
The Aspen Institute

Note: Titles and affiliations are as of the date of the conference.

About the Author

Rob Frieden serves as professor of telecommunications at Pennsylvania State University where he teaches courses in management, law, and economics. He also provides legal, management, and market forecasting consultancy services in such diverse fields as personal and mobile communications, satellites, and international telecommunications business development. Mr. Frieden has written several books, published dozens of articles in academic journals and provided commentary in a variety of trade periodicals. In 1999, Mr. Frieden and three colleagues completed a ten-year project culminating in the publication of a three volume comprehensive on communications law.

Before accepting an academic appointment, Mr. Frieden served as deputy director of International Relations for Motorola Satellite Communications, Inc. In this capacity, he provided a broad range of business development, strategic planning, policy analysis, and regulatory functions for the Iridium mobile satellite venture.

Mr. Frieden has held senior policy making positions in international telecommunications at the Federal Communications Commission and the National Telecommunications and Information Administration. In the private sector, he practiced law in Washington, D.C., and served as assistant general counsel at PTAT System, Inc. where he handled corporate, transactional, and regulatory issues for the nation's first private underseas fiber optic cable company.

Mr. Frieden holds a B.A., with distinction, from the University of Pennsylvania (1977) and a J.D. from the University of Virginia (1980).

The Aspen Institute Communications and Society Program

The overall goal of the Communications and Society Program is to promote integrated, thoughtful, values-based decision making in the fields of communications, media, and information policy. In particular, the Program focuses on the implications of communications and information technologies on democratic institutions, individual behavior, instruments of commerce, and community life.

The Communications and Society Program accomplishes this goal through two main types of activities. First, it brings together leaders of industry, government, the nonprofit sector, media organizations, the academic world, and others for roundtable meetings to explore the political, economic, and societal impact of communications and information infrastructures. Second, the Program promotes research and distributes conference reports to local, national, and global decision makers in the communications and information fields, and to the public at large.

Topics addressed by the Program vary as issues and the policy environment evolve. In recent years, the Communications and Society Program has chosen to focus on the issues of Internet policy, electronic commerce, information literacy, digital broadcasting, international and domestic telecommunications regulation, journalism, the role of the media in democratic society, and the impact of new communications technologies on democratic institutions and practices.

Charles M. Firestone has served as executive director of The Aspen Institute's Communications and Society Program for the past 10 years. In 1998, he was also named executive vice president for policy programs and international activities at the Institute. In this role, Mr. Firestone oversees the Institute's portfolio of 15 policy programs and guides the Institute's relationships with its international partners in France, Italy, Germany, and Japan. Prior to his position with The Aspen Institute, Mr. Firestone was director of the Communications Law Program at the University of California at Los Angeles and an adjunct professor at the UCLA Law School. Mr. Firestone's career includes service as an attorney at the Federal Communications Commission, as director of litigation for a Washington, D.C. based public interest law firm, and as a communications and entertainment attorney in Los Angeles. He has argued several landmark communications cases before the United States Supreme Court and other federal appellate courts. Mr. Firestone holds degrees from Amherst College and Duke University Law School, and is the editor or coauthor of seven books. He is frequently invited to speak at interactive conferences on the issues of democracy in the digital age.

Previous Publications from the Aspen Institute Roundtable on International Telecommunications

The Internet and Global Telecommunications: Exploring the Boundaries of International Coordination

Michael J. Kleeman, rapporteur. This report of the fourth annual Aspen Institute Roundtable on International Telecommunications considers appropriate roles for the public and private sectors in coordinating international decisions on Internet governance, network architecture, commerce transactions, and content regulation. 1999, 38 pages, ISBN Paper: 0-89843-266-9 $12.00

Toward Sustainable Competition in Global Telecommunications: From Principle to Practice

William J. Drake, rapporteur. This report of the third annual Aspen Institute Roundtable on International Telecommunications examines the impact of institutional arrangements on the international telecommunications landscape, e.g., the World Trade Organization, the General Agreement on Trade in Services, and the shift toward a new competitive international framework for telecommunications services. 1999, 125 pages, ISBN Paper: 0-89843-258-8 $12.00

Bits Across Borders: Policy Choices for International Multimedia and Digital Service

Kenneth G. Robinson, rapporteur. This report of the second annual Aspen Institute Roundtable on International Telecommunications focuses on the need to develop regulatory policies to support the emergence of multimedia services. Demand trends, pricing, technological considerations, regulatory and legal issues are discussed in global and country-specific context. 1997, 57 pages, ISBN Paper: 0-89843-208-1 $10.00

Building a Global Information Society

Kenneth G. Robinson, rapporteur. This report of the first annual Aspen Institute Roundtable on International Telecommunications explores national and international telecommunications policies appropriate in an era of globally integrated communications technology. The report aims to reconcile conflicting European, American, and Asian perspectives on the emerging global information infrastructure. 1996, 80 pages, ISBN Paper: 0-89843-189-1 $10.00